Y0-BRF-715

Harnessing the

Wind

Mc Graw Hill **SRA**

Columbus, OH

SRAonline.com

 SRA

Send all inquiries to this address:
SRA/McGraw-Hill
4400 Easton Commons
Columbus, OH 43219

ISBN: 978-0-07-608741-9
MHID: 0-07-608741-7

2 3 4 5 6 7 8 9 NOR 13 12 11 10 09

The McGraw-Hill Companies

What Is a Windmill?

You probably have been aware of the wind from the time you were very young. You feel it on your face. You watch the tree branches sway in it and hear it whistling around your school. But did you know that wind can be used to make power?

Today wind power is used to create electricity. But people have used windmills to harness the wind's power for centuries. Early windmills had sails that stretched out from a wheel near the top of a tower. Wind pushed the sails. This rotated a shaft that ran from the wheel down into the tower. The moving shaft pumped water or turned a stone to grind grain.

Early Windmills

Long before windmills were invented, though, a discovery was made. Around 5000 B.C., Egyptians found that they could use sails to catch the wind. The wind helped propel their boats along the Nile River.

Windmills were invented sometime around 200 B.C. The Chinese used them to pump water. People in Persia, in what is now Iran, and other parts of the Middle East used them to grind grain. Early Persian windmills looked like revolving doors. They were made of bundles of reeds fastened to a frame. By A.D. 1200, many windmills had been built across Europe, Asia, and the Middle East.

Persian Windmill

Dutch Windmill

By the 1600s the Dutch had become experts at using windmills. Their windmills did not look like the Persian ones. Instead they were made of cloth or wooden sails that turned on a wheel. The Dutch used windmills mainly to drain lakes or swampy land that was below sea level. The Dutch also used windmills to bring water to their crops.

Some Dutch windmills, called gristmills, were used to grind grain. Ones that cut wood were called sawmills. The shaft in a sawmill turned a sharp blade that cut trees into boards.

Windmill Improvements

Have you ever held a pinwheel and watched it spin in the wind? Pinwheels are like tiny colorful windmills. If a pinwheel faces the wind, it spins better.

Europeans figured out that windmills, like pinwheels, worked better if they directly faced the wind. So they built windmills called postmills. Postmills sat on wooden platforms that could be turned.

Smock mills were an improvement on postmills. Instead of turning the whole mill to catch the wind, people turned only the very top, where the sails were. The rest of the smock mill was fastened to the ground. Such buildings were better able to withstand storms.

The English used fantails to turn smock mills automatically. A fantail was made of small blades fastened to a wheel at the back of a smock mill. If the wind changed direction, the fantail swung and moved the sails of the smock mill to face the wind.

In the mid-1700s, the English discovered that angling the sails of a windmill helped them catch more wind. The English also built windmills with wooden sails that looked like window blinds. If the wind was too strong, a spring inside such a mill opened the "blinds" to slow down the sails. This kept the windmill from being damaged by high winds.

Smock mill

A windmill water pump

Windmills and Wind Turbines

For centuries windmills drained and irrigated land, sawed wood, and ground grain. They helped people make paper and grind ingredients for medicines. European immigrants built windmills when they came to America too. Germans built the first sawmill in New England in 1623. Ten years later the Dutch began building windmills in New Amsterdam, in what is now New York City.

As the young country grew, Americans used windmills to pump water to farms and to indoor plumbing, as well as to provide water for steam railroad trains. Like the Dutch, they also used windmills to saw wood and grind grain.

In the 1890s, people in Denmark began using a new kind of windmill called a wind turbine. This technology is still used today. A wind turbine makes electricity. When the wind turns the blades of the turbine, the blades spin a shaft. The shaft spins a magnet around a wire or a coil of wires. This spinning makes electricity. Wires can then carry the currents of electricity to buildings.

When wind turbines were introduced in America in the early 1900s, they were popular in rural areas. Electrical wires did not spread into those areas, so farms had no electricity unless the wind was used.

The Winds of Change

In later years the use of wind turbines shifted in a different direction. During the Great Depression in the 1930s, many banks closed. Families lost all their money. There was a long drought. Farmers did not have enough water to grow food. Many Americans were very poor during this time and could not find work.

In the early 1940s President Franklin D. Roosevelt created new programs so people would have jobs. One program brought power lines to rural areas. When that happened farmers and ranchers did not need wind turbines for electricity anymore.

After the end of World War II in 1945, wind turbines became even less popular. At that time it was cheaper and more reliable to burn fossil fuels to get electricity than to use wind turbines. Fossil fuels are oil, coal, and natural gas.

Fossil fuels were cheap through the 1960s, but their price started going up in the 1970s. People began to look for new ways of making electricity. As a result, they rediscovered an "old" way to make electricity: wind power. The use of wind turbines increased again.

Oil rigs like this
one remove
fossil fuels from
the earth.

11

A wind farm

Wind Farms

Today most electricity in the United States is still produced from fossil fuels. But many people are turning to wind turbines for electricity. These wind turbines are mounted on very tall towers. Most of them have two or three blades. They look like airplane propellers. Some turbines are shaped like eggbeaters. Sometimes many wind turbines are built in the same place to form wind farms.

Wind farms stand in places that receive strong wind all year, such as coastlines, flat ground like prairies, and mountain passes.

A wind turbine

These farms are being built all over the world. They are already creating enough electricity to power ten million homes. That number will likely increase soon.

In North America wind farms can be found from Vermont to California and from Texas to Canada. American energy organizations and others worldwide have taken a growing interest in ways to harness the wind and in places to do it. Maps that show areas with the strongest and steadiest wind have been created. These maps point out the best places to build wind farms.

The Future of Wind Farms

Wind power has many advantages. For one thing, it is renewable. Scientists think that one day the world will run out of fossil fuels. It takes millions of years for Earth to form fossil fuels, so we cannot get more of them when they are gone. The wind, on the other hand, will never run out. Also, fossil fuels pollute the air when they are burned, but wind power is clean. Harnessing wind does not harm the ecosystem as drilling for oil does. Finally, electricity made by wind power is economical because it is cheaper to produce.

Some people think that wind power is not the answer to our energy problems. They say it is unreliable. In some places the wind can be gusty at times, but at other times there is no wind at all. Some people feel that wind farms spoil the beauty of open spaces and that the hundreds of turbines are too loud. Scientists have been working on these problems by improving technology and putting wind farms in remote locations.

The world's population is growing faster and faster. More people means there will be a need for more electricity. So although the future of wind power is difficult to predict, it just might be bright!

Vocabulary

propel (prə pel´) (page 4) *v.* To cause to move forward.

currents (kûr´ ənts) (page 9) *n.* Plural form of **current:** A flow of electricity.

fossil fuels (fôs´ əl fyo͞o´ əls) (page 10) *n.* Plural of **fossil fuel:** A fuel formed from the remains of plants and animals. Coal and petroleum are fossil fuels.

ecosystem (ē´ kō sis´ təm) (page 14) *n.* All the living and nonliving things in a certain area.

economical (ek´ ə nôm´ i kəl) (page 14) *adj.* A good use of resources; not wasteful.

gusty (gus´ tē) (page 14) *adj.* Blowing in strong, sudden bursts.

predict (pri dikt´) (page 15) *v.* To tell beforehand.

Comprehension Focus: Sequence

1. List three events in the history of wind power in the order in which they happened.

2. List the steps of how a wind turbine generates electricity.